WONDROUS NATURE MANDALAS

A COLORING BOOK WITH A HIDDEN PICTURE TWIST

Jo Taylor

DOVER PUBLICATIONS, INC.
MINEOLA, NEW YORK

There are **167** hidden objects in these coloring pages!

Have fun finding them...

Caterpillars (12) Ant (10) Beetle (9)

Apples (9) Key (13) Peacock Feather (8)

Spider (5) Snail Shell (8) Owl Feather (9)

Spoons (14) Teacup (8) Woodpecker Feather (7)

Acorn (13) Bee (12) Wasp (7)

Ladybug (8) Mushrooms (10) Four Leafed Clover (5)

Bibliographical Note
Wondrous Nature Mandalas: A Coloring Book with a Hidden Picture Twist is a new work,
first published by Dover Publications, Inc., in 2016.

International Standard Book Number
ISBN-13: 978-0-486-80748-5
ISBN-10: 0-486-80748-7

Manufactured in the United States by LSC Communications
80748702 2018
www.doverpublications.com

SOLUTIONS

1. Woodpecker feather, wasp (2), beetle (2), snail shell

2. Spider, spoon (2), bee, ant

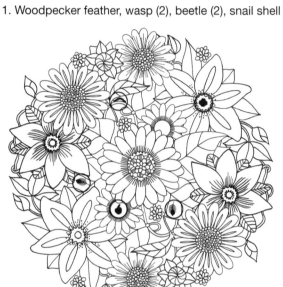

3. Caterpillar, apple, peacock feather (2), four-leaf clover

4. Ladybug (2), key, four-leaf clover (2)

5. Mushroom (2), snail shell, teacup (2), beetle

6. Spoon (2), key (2), snail shell, apple, acorn

7. Owl feather (2) acorn (2), ant, key

8. Woodpecker feather (2), spider, peacock feather, bee

9. Caterpillar (2), wasp, owl feather

10. Caterpillar, peacock feather (2), bee (2), acorn

11. Snail shell (2), acorn (2), spoon (2)

12. Teaspoon, teacup (2), mushroom, acorn, apple

13. Woodpecker feather (2), beetle (2), owl feather, teacup

14. Mushroom, ladybug (2), spider, apple (2), acorn

15. Caterpillar, ant (2), key, mushroom (2)

16. Bee (2), owl feather, wasp, ant, spider

17. Wasp (2), four-leaf clover, ladybug (2), spider

18. Spoon (2), key (3), caterpillar (2)

19. Caterpillar, apple, mushroom (2), bee

20. Bee (2), caterpillar (2), acorn

21. Caterpillar (2), spoon, ant, woodpecker feather, owl feather

22. Acorn, apple (2), spoon (3)

23. Owl feather (2), bee, snail shell (2), key, ladybug

24. Ladybug, peacock feather (3), beetle, ant

25. Wasp, key (2), teacup, acorn (3)

26. Mushroom (2), bee (2), woodpecker feather, spoon, four-leaf clover

27. Ant, beetle (3), owl feather, key (2)

28. Apple, snail shell, ant (2), teacup (2)